Confini:

Poems of Refugees in Sicily

Michelle Reale

Červená Barva Press
Somerville, Massachusetts

Červená Barva Press
P.O. Box 440357
W. Somerville, MA 02144-3222

www.cervenabarvapress.com

Bookstore: www.thelostbookshelf.com

Cover art: "Portal" by Michelle Reale

Cover design: William J. Kelle

ISBN: 978-1950063-25-3

ACKNOWLEDGMENTS

To Ramzi Harrabi: much gratitude and much love for your time, companionship, and mentoring: I couldn't have done it without you. To Olivia Kate Cerrone: thank you for believing in the work. To Warren Haffar: thank you so much for providing the opportunity and for always being a champion. To colleagues Alex Otieno and Jennifer Riggan: your support has made the world of difference. To Chad Frame, your sensitive and sharp eye saved me. To Jeanne Buckley for listening. To Susi Kimbell, Franca Lupo, Lucia Ortisi, Ros Belford, Elizabeth Atkinson, Sarah Milthorpe, and Hannah Milthorpe: *mille grazie*, for your deep, deep friendship, many delicious meals, and hospitality beyond anything I deserve. You all held me up. Words cannot express my gratitude. To the many refugees whose stories I attempted to tell: thank you for opening your hearts and lives when you had nothing to gain from it. *I will never forget you.*

Grateful acknowledgement is given to the following journals where some of these poems first appeared: *Cultural Studies* ←→ *Critical Methodologies, Journal of Contemporary Ethnography, The Qualitative Report, Qualitative Inquiry and International Review of Qualitative Research.*

TABLE OF CONTENTS

ACKNOWLWDGMENTS

FORWARD

ABOUT THE AUTHOR

For Mody Awad Awad

Wanderer, the road is your footsteps, nothing else;
wanderer, path there is none,
only tracks on ocean foam.

~ **Antonio Machado,** *Proverbias y Cantares*

"...exile is strangely compelling to think about but terrible to experience. It is the unhealable rift forced between a human being and a native place, between the self and its true home: its essential sadness can never be surmounted. And while it is true that literature and history contain heroic, romantic, glorious, even triumphant episodes in an exile's life, these are no more than efforts meant to overcome the crippling sorrow of estrangement."

~ **Edward Said, Reflections on Exile and Other Essays**

"In this world, shipmates, sin that pays its way can travel freely, and without a passport; whereas Virtue, if a pauper, is stopped at all frontiers."

~ **Herman Melville, Moby Dick**

The Mediterranean Sea has turned into a cemetery for transgressive travelers, and the floating dead bodies washing upon the shores of European tourist islands are evidence of border-necropolitics.

~ **Sharam Khosravi,** *Illegal Traveller: An Auto-Ethnography of Borders.*

FOREWORD

by Alex Otieno

Refuge?

Recent and old-time refugee stories

Encapsulate memories, longing, hope, despair and defiance

Futures of possible freedom

Unyielding complexity confounded by obvious simplification of the comings and

Goings and teaching and learning and

Even dignity

Everything before, in between and after

Stories of refugees are more than a tapestry

In their poetry and encounters with them

No one tells the refugee story like those with lived experience of refuge

Suleiman, Shereef, Hussain, Tibia, Muhammad, Musa, Essa, and many others

In this collection represent diverse attitudes and offer divergent

Counter narratives to limited stories of the refugee and notions of refuge

In myriad ways, the poet captures their everyday lives within and beyond

Liminal experiences of: working, loving, hoping, regaling, dancing and singing, summoning

Yesterday, today, and tomorrow, the flow: arrivals, waiting, detention, and unknown futures…

Professor Alex Otieno, a native of Kenya, has taught at Arcadia since 2001. He earned a Master's Degree from Temple University and is completing a PhD at the University of South Africa. His research interests are in public health, human rights, and human services. Professor Otieno teaches a broad range of courses, including Introductory Sociology, Ethnographic Film and courses on HIV/AIDS and homelessness.

Confini:

Poems of Refugees in Sicily

Civics Class for Refugees, Sicily

This room is all blue   green hues   when we
enter the colors bleed into one another   These men   submerged
in each other's shadows,   gesticulating in circles like small
nations   outside red-tailed hawks screech like seagulls.
close your eyes   you could be on a beautiful beach   only
you are not   iron bars embrace square holes in the wall
What are they keeping in?   What are they keeping out?
All this black skin   *azzurro* walls   ironed shirts and
aftershave   shards of glass on the pavement   will
start the inferno   because this sun will set everything ablaze
Lesson one: let's compare our skin colors   I might be able to tell
each of you how to further contort your already stretched bodies
becoming pliable is the goal   we learn quick, don't we?
forget your mother's milk   your father's grain culled from
the land of your ancestors   your grandfather's proud gold
tooth   try to forget that small boat.   that dark
night   let's add a layer of comfort here   we will thank
you for your extreme attention,   because we know our
words are like shiny bullets grazing your ears.   Lesson two:
all sores heal eventually   we've seen it before when we all
leave this room   lungs will expand with relief
cigarettes   will be lit   The *storno nero*[1] will   screech
only to get your collective attention   they circle only to
welcome you   please know this:

it is not an omen, but   only   just.

---

[1] Black starling

3

Suleiman

Can someone please tell me the meaning of *accoglienza²* and *integrazione³* for the immigrato? Just send me back on the street for the sake of Allah. My mother would hold her head in her hands *all the day* if she knew of my life like this. They tell me to leave the center and stuff 500 Euro in my pocket. But that money cannot buy me the only thing that I want: a job. My cap is the only roof over my head. Even *it* has a job. Outside, I do not know If the heat is worse than the cold. The same *polizia⁴* stops me every day at the water pump. Every day, I show him my same ID card. Every day, he examines my old plastic container. Every day, I swallow more pride like a disfigured gourd in my throat. Every day, the people in this town begrudge me some water to wet my tongue. Every day, the *polizia* says to me *mossa⁵!* Sometimes, he calls me *fratello⁶*.

---

² Hospitality
³ Integration
⁴ Police
⁵ Move
⁶ Brother

Shereef

When the boat arrived, my body was pulled to the shore. Squinting eyes looked into my face and I blinked back at them. 'This one is alive,' they said, as if I were not there like a fish still on the hook. If I could breathe and walk, they left me and went on to the next person. In Afghanistan, they shot a hole in my chest but missed my heart, which, in turn, missed the lack of attention. Hearts are fickle that way. They should have taken all of me. Because I will not talk because they think I cannot remember who I am or where I may have come from. They do not speak to me. I am on a stretcher, transported as if I am a box of summer vegetables. Only once, I hear someone say *attento, attento*[7]. I have never slept on sheets so white, a floor so shiny. A woman with a serious look on her face brings me food on a tray. I want to know her name. But really if I could find my voice, I would try to smile and call her mother so that I never lose the sound of the word on my lips.

---

[7] Careful, careful

Hussain

At the time we were the
first refugees to be officially
recognized, but they forgot
our laurel wreaths. Now what?
They told me here is your *permesso di soggiorno*[8]
and I looked around me at
faces with no smiles,
tired before I even began.
I quickly realized the only
difference between this place
and Libya was that there was
no war with big guns.
I had discrimination in Libya
but soon I was dreaming in
that old nostalgic way of returning
and living my Libyan experience again.
Here, on the streets, they look at me
and look away. Sometimes I look away first.

---

[8] Temporary residence permit controlled by the Polizia di Stato.

Fifteen days on the water
and the silence of two broken engines
nearly made me lose my mind.
The only sound was of a Ghanaian woman,
wrapped in the cloth of her country,
moaning with a baby in her belly.
I could only stare. We were all so helpless.
I had a wet cigarette in my pocket
and not a single match to light it with.

Their Heads Upon Stones

How do you think I feel? I have just slept in a room with fifteen other women. Her silky scar conceals what one might imagine to be thick, dark hair, its colorful pattern revealing the life she lived before *l'approdo,* the landing. Another life, but not here. Her small, round hand rests on her still, flat belly, her eyes appropriately downcast. Her soft touch signals a beginning. *Eight hours in the hospital and not one person spoke to me. But then they tell me the baby is okay—but I am not.* Her father raises his hand, and she is silenced. He will walk as far as he needs to for green vegetables. He does not know where he will go, but somewhere beyond the camp. As yet unaccustomed to the national dish, the threads of pasta make them cringe. The men rub their bloodshot eyes, light gold-tipped ubiquitous cigarettes. The flies hover over this human circle in abundance. *We are crowned in wreaths of smoke.* Banal clucks of sympathy are sparse, signaling nothing useful. *I cannot eat your emotions,* the father spits. His daughter's husband is in a country where they are still cowering in corners. *We will send word,* he says inside the circle, to which no one responds. What will the word be? The father exhales a miasma of cigarette smoke straight as a missile. The hands that hold the unfiltered cigarette shake.
Inshallah[9].

---

[9] Godwilling

Tibia Plays in the Refugee Camp

She likes to play mommy. But first, she colors the picture she has drawn. A small boat on a big sea, surrounded by curly, cartoon waves. The waves have eyes--thick, angry eyebrows. Her little brother tries to grab her paper, his small hands opening and closing. She smacks him hard, intones the voice of her missing mother, shakes her pudgy little finger with chipped orange polish in his face. He cries, running into the arms of an Italian relief worker, who tries to console him while holding him at a distance. She goes back to her picture, starts outlining the waves in blue and green. The flies are persistent, landing on her nose, eyelashes, and the many braids in her hair. She sighs, puts down her crayon, and picks it up again. The men from Mali, their backs against the chain link fence, watch her with vacant eyes. She gazes at them, sitting like sentries. A whine turns quickly to a sob. The scattered clouds are iron-grey, holding, blending with the concrete. A woman who is not Tibia's mother shuffles by, dragging her feet in her rubber slippers. Tibia begins to say her own name over and over again, as if trying to remember who she is. She goes back to her drawing. Adds stick figures to the boat. They all have their stick arms up in the air. Alarm. All of their round, broken heads have mouths that are large. *Red and agape.*

Exodus and Requiem

The boat drifts in the gloaming.
No room for the needed insulin.
Reassurances with the gleam of a gold tooth.
You will arrive before you know it. Imagine.
You cannot generate a future from a body bag.
The darkness envelopes everything
 when the sun is not blinding you.
Soon, out of necessity, survivors will learn new things:
how to politicize a death:
invite the mayor,
a politician,
an imam,
a broad-minded priest.
An archbishop in solemn robes presides
among the faithful, adding the appropriate
dose of gravitas.
Forget caritas.
Here, the men know what to do with the
dead body of a young woman.
Insert a bit of Arabic.
Murmur appropriate outrage. Act like you mean it.
Fare bella figura[10].
Here are misbegotten contracts of
highly charged situations.
Her father arrived with her, but is now
gone in search of his new home.
The white van with the
German license plates will take him there.

---

[10] Make a good impression.

He leaves her to the indifference of strangers.
Her stiff body lies in the *Duomo*,
so far from where she has come from.
Strangers puzzle over her death
with morbid fascination.
Tourists take photos of the ceremony,
lick their *gelati*[11], eventually move on.
To the well-dressed women sweating in their thick makeup,
benedictions and speeches are blessedly short.
Afterwards, watch them refresh their bright lipstick
on grim mouths and
light their long brown cigarettes.

---

[11] Ice cream

Abito[12]

My mentor's forehead gleams in the unforgiving sun. He has no words. *Lampedusa*[13] hangs like an iron weight on our bowed backs; in our hearts, and in our minds. He brushes the lapels of the suit jacket that he specifically *did not* purchase for the funeral. Not for *this* funeral. Wonders at his luck, to have a suit just in time, as if serendipitous things still happened in the world. Knows he will have use of it again and again. All the things in this world that you can safely depend upon.

---

[12] Suit.

[13] One of the Pelagie islands in the Mediterranean sea. On 3 October 2013, a boat carrying migrants from Libya to Italy sank off the Italian island of Lampedusa. Over 360 people , including men, women and children were confirmed dead.

Ab Ovo[14]

His voice is deep, rising, sinking. The long, thin body carries the sweet smell of cologne and sweat. It folds in on itself, draping the metal folding chair. American students listen hard. He tells them of the journey on a boat that looked like the broken back of an old man moments from death. Now he lives in a country that hates him and that he hates in return. *Don't look at me like that! Do you think I just fell out of a tree?* A miasma of collective breath is held in suspension. He tugs downward on his cap, holds up a large, soft hand with a pale palm. Whispers in the language of the oppressor: *perdonami*[15].

---

[14] From the very beginning.
[15] Forgive me.

Pomodori

Do you know where Nardo is? In Puglia?
I am waiting to harvest the *pomodori*.
I cannot stay in Sicilia.
Do not worry about me!
We are many men together just waiting for the *pomodori*[16].

---

[16] Tomatoes.

Veni Qua[17]

The kitten's name is *Veni Qua*. They live together in a house with
no roof. Abandoned. He calls to the cat like a lullaby, *veni qua, veni
qua*. The local woman with the limp and milky eye feeds her little
balls of *pane*[18], pinches the *pulci*[19] between her fingernails.
Sometimes pasta on a cracked plate reserved for the abundant
strays. The locals respect the itinerant nature of cats. Muhammad
thinks it's easier to be a cat in Sicily than it is to be a refugee.
Veni[20], he calls, holding out a trembling hand.
Veni, he repeats, until he no longer recognizes the sound of the
foreign language coming out of his own mouth.

---

[17] Come here.
[18] Bread
[19] Fleas
[20] Come

Lavoro[21]

I have no contract. I will take the job others do not want. Every day I show up and ask the *padrone*[22] : Is this the day I can work? I pray in the language of the Italians he will say *yes*. I will lay out the big plastic blue sheets and wash them all day long while I lick my own sweat. I will be careful to step away from the long snakes coiled and ready to spring from the field.

---

[21] Work.
[22] Literally "master." Boss.

Chi Sono?[23]

I came from a family just like you did.
I have a mother, who loves me, at least.
Rome might be a better place. It sounds like a question.
He knows of the cardboard houses, fragile as a house of cards,
the men who knife each other in the streets.
I need to work, he repeats often, like a mantra.
A father who is no more, but I was his own.
His voice holds a serrated edge, and yet, he is a gentleman.
Do you know who I am?
I am Muhammad.
An almost imperceptible
Movement of his hand
Across his eyes, his face.
There are many of us. I am just one among them.
But really, tell me please: who am I here, so far from home?

---

[23] Who am I

Sgradito[24]

I see him on the street first. I wave. I am polite. I congratulate myself on my civility as I wait 15 minutes after he fumbles at the door of the Internet point with his big ring of keys. I sip my espresso and sweat in the sun while I think of how I might approach Ibrahim to know something of his life. I think how good it will be to see him in his element: *The Internet Point.*
I walk in and smile. From behind his little booth he bares his teeth. I flush the incarnadine of the unwelcome. Several Eritrean men, tall, lanky and hollow-eyed, wear the football jerseys of Palermo, Catania, Lazio like the unofficial patriots of their new home. They sprawl on metal chairs waiting to use the only two computers staring at me, then at Ibrahim. *Back and forth.*
I am so sick of you white people with your notebooks and microphones! Who do you think you are? You come to my place of business where I work hard, where I make my money and you want me to tell a fairy tale or a story of hard luck. Get out! He yells.
My feet stick to the floor.

Sgradito! Sgradito! Sgradito!

How does it feel, he asks as a parting shot with a toothy smile, sharp and pointy like concertina wire.

---

[24] Unwelcome.

Musa

This is my story. Let me unfurl it the way that I want to. I am a proud *Susu*[25] from Guinea but the Italian people have fueled my great, great delusion. Do not even talk to me of hopes and dreams. What are they? Listen to my story carefully: I vowed never to repeat myself in this new place. I will say what I have to say only once.

---

[25] A Mandé ethnic group living primarily in Guinea

Nessuno Stato[26]

One year in a camp and no mediation for my condition. Don't act surprised! You know the game here. They could find no one who could speak to me in the tongue of my mother. I was given one year of protection owed to me by law. I have been here for five years, and I am proud, but still, I have no status. I am nothing and going nowhere.

---

[26] No state.

Senzatetto[27]

I have no home. No conscription in the *Servizio Sanitario Nazionale*[28]. I had terrible pain in my kidneys. *Yow!* I used to yell *all the night.* I went to the police and said *help me please.* They laughed at me. They said: *do we look like doctors?* I went to the hospital where I waited three hours for nothing. They sent me home. I am 26 years old but this white hair on my head tells you more than my words. Am I right? And still, I yell *Yow!* in the night.

---

[27] Homeless.
[28] Italy's National Health Service

Bicicletta[29]

When I came to Italy, I met a woman. I loved her. Then I found out there were three men before me. I did not want to be number four. A man sold me a bike. This *bicicletta* is like my wife. She is mine and no one else can have her. I like to ride my *bicicletta* but sometimes I think: *what if I fall?* I tell myself: *I have fallen before; I will get up again.*

---

[29] Bicycle.

Una Storia Semplice[30]

I never wanted to come to Italy. I had no particular place in mind, I just wanted to save my own life. *My goal was me and me and me.* It is not easy to live here on the edge, but really, one does not have a choice. I acknowledge all who have done good things for me, and I believe the Lord will put good people in my way. But the way things are now, no one depends on me, and I depend on no one. It is better that way.

---

[30] A simple story.

Passage

That iron, unbreakable faith is misplaced from the beginning: that boat is not a seaworthy vessel. That man is not your father, not your brother. The money you hand over, touching palms as though it really means something, does not make a contract of safe passage. Trees, sun, sand, home, skeleton key, and village elders will be soon replaced with cement, salt water, and indifference. That is not sweat. Those are tears. Here comes the feel of a boot on the back of your neck, whether real or imagined. Hear the intonation of your own parched voice whispering like a mantra: *why, why, why?*

The Half Life of Boats

The boats are tethered to the dock, undeserving, even, of proper nautical knots. Here lies the evidence of those who travel light not out of conviction, but cruel necessity. Someone is, apparently, negotiating his new home with one shoe, the ever-hopeful without his striped tie, without the packets of Syrian tea waterlogged amidst the shit, the plastic bottles, the coat shed due to the heat, the cold, the dark, or the confusion. The boats bob lightly, swaying in the sea breeze. Like the sad pieces of refuse they are, their job is done. What remains is the corrosion, the leaks, and ash. The rust is alive. It proliferates. The smell is indistinguishable to the uninitiated from the spill of blood from open veins, from the breaking of hearts, the dry rot of hope from the crude excision of everything that came before.

Welcome/Reception

Do not protest the separation of
the parents from children,
the young from the old
the merely sick from the dying.
Smile at the guards, grim-faced officials
swilling their coffee.
Ignore the firearms strapped
to their tense arm muscles, their bulging thighs.
Ignore their large, open pores, the extreme heat,
their controlled, but taut and tired patience.
Perform your role.
Be sad, but not too sad.
Gratitude will go a long way.
Keeping eyes downcast is a strategy that,
anecdotally, has been a success
in the past.
Ask all the right questions:
How long can I stay?
Can I call this place home?
Think carefully before answering theirs:
Why do you come? Where will you go? When will you leave.

Dancing in the Refugee Camp at Dusk

The men shake
and twist their long, thin
limbs to Bob Marley,
patron saint of the struggle.

The tips of their cigarettes
ignite the velvet darkness
as Bob Marley fades
and the Arabic music begins.
On stage, the singer scans the crowd,
poised to please.

Arms fly heavenward,
fists held aloft in solidarity
toward a God who, finally,
speaks their language;
who understands them.

Cell phones record this moment
out of time, *click, click, click.*
This to my Ma,
this to my brother.
They laugh at their slack muscle tone
and wipe at their shiny faces,
slick with sweat
despite the cold air.

The trilling and dancing
punctures the thick membrane
of dull boredom, stubborn despair,
the fog of what they still
do not know, but what
haunts them anyway.

When the music begins to die,
great thanks is given both to Jesus
and Allah, but they want more.
The Arabic singer calms them,

his throat is parched. *Be grateful, please,*
he tells them.

They carry themselves to their rooms
or stand in the courtyard,
reluctant for it all to end,
humming Bob Marley,
thanking Allah.
Keeping it strong.

Backs Against the Wall

The men who stand alone
are the ones who want
to talk the most.
In the camp, it is dangerous
not to have any friends.
To be a lone wolf will
mark you as prey.
Keep your back against the wall.
Essa stands with hands
Stuffed into the pockets of his
too large coat.
Do you know Senegal?
Yes, I tell him. *Yes.*
He laughs.
What do you know, tell me!
I say nothing and he snorts.
He doesn't even know where to begin.
I am tired, he says.
His eyes are red.
He rubs the back of his neck,
like an old man who has already
lived his life.
Still, he tries to make an impression,
shows me photos.
I'm hanging with my boys.
He tells me that back home
He was all sculpted muscle,
upturned chin, confident.
I can see it.
He sucks his teeth as if in pain.
He closes his eyes, then
is when he opens them
is surprised that I am still there.
Ah, you see, my mother, he starts
though his voice drifts away.
He balls his hands into fists.
I think he knows I understand.
It is all I have to offer.

The Life of a Humble Prince

This is thug life?
Well, yes, this is thug life.
Self-style who you want to be,
the person that will keep you alive.
Let me tell you something:
we conserve energy here
or else we would be hungry
all the time.
We only look lazy, but we aren't.
This will make me a man, a man.
Do you understand me?
This will be a better life.
I am a thug, ya man. (ha ha ha)
I say to my boy, *You fat, man.*
Word up.
Si, si, me say ya man.
Thanks for every little thing.
Ya, don't worry.
Sometimes the food is enough.
My mother used to make me food
with her own two hands.
But no, man, I tell you true,
it is never enough.
Here is a big game,
big, big camp, but hard going.
I tell you true.
I am going good, yo.
Keeping it strong.
Every day, doing what I can.

Leaving Umberto I[31]

They begin to circle like blackbirds. One tosses his
cigarette, too tired to inhale, exhale. Shoulders hunched,
baggage in heaps where one old woman watches like
a sentry.

The women wear somber headscarves in the heat. One girl holds a
wedding dress, buries her face in the rough lace. Animated
Arabic mixes with dialect and the smiles of the *carabinieri*[32] are tight,
their patience worn thin as a communion wafer.

The road outside of the high iron like steel jaws awaits, but it
entices those who want to leave the country to go on
to meet other relatives who survived the journey.

We are told to turn our heads, to look away. The guards
with their guns turn their heads; some cross themselves.
They begin the sad march to who knows where. A path
strewn with malignant thorns. Soon, a new alphabet for all.

---

[31] Refugee camp in Sicily
[32] Italian military force

Bandiera[33]

Revolutions are made by the people. Here is my story—not that old one. I have another. The wind blows so hard my words are not very clear, and my tongue wraps around itself when you look at me in that way.

The last sense of peace I had was in my mother's belly. This has not been a trip of pleasure. Flying that flag was harder than I thought, wrought with all manner of complications.

I rested my arms for the amount of time it took to replace one large-fisted leader with another. Before I knew it, the whole fragile mansion came crashing down, one room on top of another, but no witnesses would ever come forth.

Words go subterranean, even though my poem may reach only a handful of people who have nothing better to do except to sigh with relief that they are resolutely uninvolved, that someone else is fighting the good fight.

Gestures can be more effective, though I haven't the slightest idea how to make the first one. My mentor has left me bereft. Everyone here goes by instinct and speaks all the fashionable languages.

My best instincts have been blunted by a lack of courage, an offense equal to treason in these parts, and still there are ethical questions that have no right or wrong answers.

Are you still listening?

Here is the real story: there are boats that are leaving the continent every single day and their families clutch bright-colored clothes, press them on their swollen eyes, touch their hearts and say *there they go!*

---

[33] Flag

We pace on our shore. Some smoke. We all wring our hands. We say, *Aieeeeee, here they come!*

We catalog what we see, we scratch details onto official reports. The shine of the eyes, the crusted salt on parched lips, the blister of the skin, the ball of the fists.

Our flag lays curled in the corner, consoling itself for lack of what they will find here, there, or anywhere at all.

Coda

The purpose of poetry is to remind us
how difficult it is to remain just one person,
for our house is open, there are no keys in the doors,
and invisible guests come in and out at will.

~ *Czeslaw Milosz, "Ars Poetica?"*

These poems are my response to the refugee crisis in Sicily that I witnessed in refugee camps, periodically, between 2011-2016. While I collected field notes over the years, I worried about how I would present this research. I have used poetic inquiry, an arts based methodology that has allowed me to present these poems in the most truthful and evocative way possible. There is no single story of any one event, and here I present poems that help to explicate, but certainly not speak for, the refugees' condition, in any complete or definitive way. In most cases, I have used the actual words of the men and women themselves. The refugee has been demonized, misrepresented, and scapegoated in Italy for a long time.

My poems attempt to pluck these brave men and women from the nameless and faceless "human tsunami" (as Berlusconi so callously called these victims of war and famine) and, with my words, create an understanding of their plight that may increase awareness and compassion and help to change restrictive and harmful policies against those who see not only a better life, but in many cases, basic survival.

I have no illusions that these poems will save the world, or even save the people I wrote them about. I am both a poet and researcher, but also a human being. I felt their sorrows intensely, feel them intensely still across space and time.

The work is humble, and I offer one representation of what I witnessed. The bravery that is entailed in leaving all that you know, every single thing familiar to you, never to see your home again, is one most Americans cannot comprehend. That so many are forced to do so is worse than a scandal. They neither need nor want our pity, our downcast eye, or our castoffs. They need understanding. Jobs. A place to live. A future.

Writing these poems and being among these men and women refugees helped me, perhaps more than them. They humbled me. The helped me to see below the surface of things, to understand how deep misfortune due to political upheaval, war or even environmental disasters, could cause any one of us to leave our homes with the clothes on our backs. Our ignorance and superiority allow us to assume we would be wanted anywhere. The absurdity of this way of thinking is beyond my comprehension, and yet, it exists.

The men and women I encountered, who happen to be refugees have uncertain futures, and yet they are not without joy. They are certainly not without hope. *The work continues.*

ABOUT THE AUTHOR

Michelle Reale is a full professor at Arcadia University. She is the author of twelve collections of poetry including *Season of Subtraction* (Bordighera Press, 2019) and *Blood Memory: Prose Poems* (Idea Press, 2021). She has twice been nominated for a Pushcart Prize.